STAG—MOOSE

by Sara Gilbert

CREATIVE EDUCATION • CREATIVE PAPERBACKS

Published by Creative Education and Creative Paperbacks
P.O. Box 227, Mankato, Minnesota 56002
Creative Education and Creative Paperbacks are
imprints of **The Creative Company**
www.thecreativecompany.us

Design and production by **Chelsey Luther**
Art direction by **Rita Marshall**
Printed in the **United States of America**

Photographs by Alamy (dieKleinert, The Natural History Museum, Stocktrek
Images, Inc., Universal Images Group North America LLC), Corbis (Brooklyn
Museum, Daniel Eskridge/Stocktrek Images), Dreamstime (Artesiawells,
Tranac), FreeVectorMaps.com, Getty Images (Dorling Kindersley, Fine Art
Photographic), Shutterstock (lynea)

Illustration on p. 12 © 2016 Michael Rothman

Library of Congress Cataloging-in-Publication Data
Gilbert, Sara.
Stag-moose / Sara Gilbert.
p. cm. — (Ice age mega beasts)
Includes bibliographical references and index.
Summary: An elementary exploration of stag-moose, focusing on fossil
evidence that helps explain how their wide antlers and sharp hooves helped
these beasts adapt to the last Ice Age.

ISBN 978-1-60818-770-6 (hardcover)
ISBN 978-1-62832-378-8 (pbk)
ISBN 978-1-56660-812-1 (eBook)
1. Deer, Fossil—Juvenile literature. 2. Mammals, Fossil—Juvenile literature.
3. Prehistoric animals.

QE882.U3 G55 2017
569.65—dc23   2016014623

CCSS: RI.1.1, 2, 3, 4, 5, 6, 7, 10; RI.2.1, 2, 4, 5, 6, 7, 10; RI.3.1, 2, 4, 5, 7, 10;
RF.1.1, 2, 3, 4; RF.2.3, 4; RF.3.3, 4

First Edition HC 9 8 7 6 5 4 3 2 1
First Edition PBK 9 8 7 6 5 4 3 2 1

Contents

Munching Moose   5

Ice Age Plant Eaters   8

Wetland Deer   13

Scary Antlers   16

Stag-moose Close-up   22

Glossary   23

Read More   24

Websites   24

Index   24

Munching Moose

It is quiet in the swamp. The bushes and trees sway in the breeze. The only sound is the gentle chewing of leaves. A huge stag-moose is eating!

Plant-eating animals are also known as herbivores.

A stag-moose looked like an elk crossed with a moose. It was bigger than today's moose. Its *antlers* were wide and flat.

stag-moose   **today's moose**   **first-grader**

Stag-moose stood about one to two feet (0.3–0.6 m) taller than today's moose.

Ice Age Plant Eaters

Stag-moose lived during the last Ice Age. They had to stay ahead of the huge sheets of ice called glaciers that moved across North America. They needed grass and plants to eat.

Ice Age glaciers

As the Ice Age ended, the stag-moose moved north again.

Stag-moose lived near other large animals. Some neighbors were giant beavers and long-horned bison. These big plant eaters had to watch out for *predators*. Dire wolves and saber-toothed cats hunted stag-moose.

Stag-moose avoided predators by running away or entering deep water.

Wetland Deer

Stag-moose lived in the woods and *wetlands* of eastern and middle North America. They moved around in search of leaves and other food.

Most stag-moose remains have been found in the American Midwest.

Stag-moose *fossils* have been found in Kentucky, Ohio, New Jersey, and Illinois. Parts of their antlers have been found in Iowa, too.

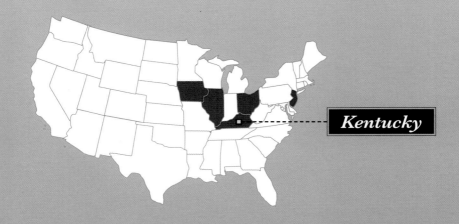

Kentucky

People found the first stag-moose fossils in Kentucky in 1805.

Scary Antlers

The stag-moose used its antlers for many things. They helped the moose pull down leafy branches to eat. They also scared away some predators.

Other deer relatives even bigger than stag-moose lived in Europe and Asia.

Stag-moose also had sharp hooves. These broke up ice and snow. Then the moose could find food underneath the ice.

Moose hooves can act as snowshoes, helping moose walk over snow.

19

As the Ice Age ended, new animals appeared. They ate the same plants as stag-moose. Humans also may have hunted stag-moose. Like other big Ice Age animals, the stag-moose died out about 11,500 years ago.

The Irish elk, which died out around 5000 B.C., was the biggest deer relative.

Stag-moose Close-up

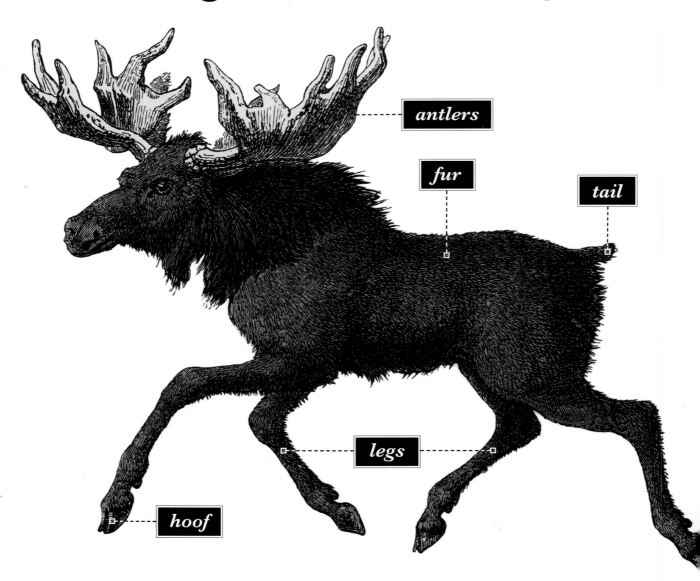

antlers

fur

tail

legs

hoof

Glossary

antlers: branched horns on top of a male moose or other deer's head; they grow and are shed every year

fossils: remains of animals or plants

predators: animals that hunt other animals for food

wetlands: swampy lands where plants grow

Read More

Lindsay, William. *Eyewitness Prehistoric Life*. New York: DK, 2012.

Turner, Alan. *National Geographic Prehistoric Mammals*. Washington, D.C.: National Geographic, 2004.

Websites

About Education: Stag Moose
http://dinosaurs.about.com/od/mesozoicmammals/p/Stag-Moose-Cervalces-Scotti.htm
Learn interesting facts about stag-moose.

Enchanted Learning: Ice Age Mammals
http://www.enchantedlearning.com/subjects/mammals/Iceagemammals.shtml
Find out more about the Ice Age and the animals that lived then.

Index

antlers **7, 15, 16**

elk **7**

food **5, 8, 13, 18, 20**

fossils **15**

glaciers **8**

hooves **18**

Ice Age **8, 20**

moose **7**

predators **10, 16**

size **7**

wetlands **5, 13**

woods **13**